I, Boombox

I, Boombox

Robert Glück

Illustrations by Colter Jacobsen

ROOF BOOKS
New York

ISBN: 978-0-937804-96-4
Library of Congress Control Number: 2022951882

Cover art: "Radio Pudding (for Joe Brainard)" by Frank Moore
Whitney Museum of American Art, New York;
gift of the Gesso Foundation

Illustrations by Colter Jacobsen

Book design by Venn Daniel

Author photo by Xavi Permanyer

This book is made possible by the New York State Council on the Arts with the support of the Office of the Governor and the New York State Legislature.

Roof Books are published by:
Segue Foundation
300 Bowery FL 2
New York, NY 10012
seguefoundation.com

Roof Books are distributed by:
Small Press Distribution
1341 Seventh Street
Berkeley, CA. 94710-1403
Phone orders: 800-869-7553
spdbooks.org

I, Boombox is fashioned from my misreadings. In that sense, it's an autobiography in which I dream on the page. It is my version of the modernist long poem: published in sections and interrupted only by the author's death.

I came wincing
in the heat. I
close my eyes or
focus on a
plan where on each
autumnal day
sunlight decreases
in the Alaskan
manner. Or a
nothing neither
form busts me like
an unemployed
prayer. Sweat beaded
glossily, he
gilded out, revealing
in glow, licensing
her to the point
of exhaustion,
or precludes a
new construction
system around
molestation.
Start a genital
uprising. How

get away with
beginning more
distant from? How
about a glass
of wine said my
mother, stepping
into her son.
“The redder the
bedder.” Caper
salad mafia-
style, or the
missing bitterness
in the words of
the sunset. A
memoir in the
environment.
In your surviving
reality
I’d like to be
briefly demoted.
History is
written by the
victims. UV
winds readdress

the brain. Let the
navy hang itself
or the artist
execute himself.
I rush into
the bellicose
grease of Bauhaus
Bahamas or
ugly non-design
manufacturers
banished from Europe.
A little more
power over
that memory
that runs from camp
to camp like Joan
of Arc, that a
shortcake announcement
Hong Kong Radio
picked up. The truth
of the asserted
attorney, or
mental image
of an octopus

stupendously
policing consciousness.
Confidentially
we'll pay for feet
in both cities
as if from now
on I could not
put a foot wrong.
He doesn't need
to make a hole
in the dark or
overstep the
tissue. Household
delusion or
I behave the
invisible
ink. Emotionally
insecured, play
with the divested
modest ceramist
or include a
description of
your condolences.
Trust and grind the

sputtering lines.
I behaved the
objects from the
autocratic
tombs, if only
inspecting the
wreckage of spirit
holding prodigious
commentary
in his cock. Licking
other planets,
burnt sugar delays
the short fifth season.
The electrical
power station
constructed the
18th Century.
Fat applies, changed
overweight from
fried to betrayer.
I felt compelled
to copulate
before what seemed
to me the insane

loquacity.
coming across
our baby in
a foreign zoo...
The Flinch Club or
The Henry Jones
Society.
A reef of essays
cuts across their
integrity
on that side of
the fetish. It
holds Annie's heart
in one pen. Often
it is said that
when XY speaks
it is without.
I cast my net,
inattention.
Here's the coast: he
grabs a breath, sex
and a half degrees.
Snoop socialist,
even in the

streets were far more
cats than people
as I stood there
decanted. The
men's channel: I
forgot to change.
Events stick. Closet
sketchpad, your two-
dimensional
brother's heart gives
sideways thumps, the
charms of ethical
love: the marriage
of the Artistic
Director and
the President
of the Boardroom.
Aliengnosis:
flatted out mind.
Or on fire to
be kissed: Plutarch.
Hippie penises
contract. I feel
the barely there

hairs glazing the
back of my neck
or my prostate's
static: the strangled
heaven of Messiaen's
orchestra: a
miracle wave
breaks into my
ears. Lashes, as
if the word by
its very nature
hates me. The reader
faced with so many
subtitles that
action scandalized
his rear end, long
spurts clawing the
air over Bill's
body. Lend your
culture to an
anonymous
subject, a pair
of disgusting
hunting dogs at

his feet or carrying
discs to his soul.
Arts-infested
long-life learner,
finger out exactly
what each man wants.
Crewlboi73
for No Strings Fun.
Firmball, Dominate
Your Vehicle.
Prada pimps its
technology,
its classical
expression of
a commercial
way of living
or believing.
A poop ballad
that floats down from
invisible
speakers. Everyone
snoozes on the
possible terrace.
California

landscape L/R.
October, have
you ever seen
anything of
a double nature?
Vintage Japan
tomb filled and please
do not open
immediately.
Excuse me, your
teeth scrape my dick,
spitting apart
the coalition
government. Sex
is a bite like
a magic spell,
something. He lifted
his t-shirt above
his nipples to
destroy them. The
bareback seraglio
has a wife and
some kids. Guilt by
disassociation.

Find vegetable
children for Chris...
Earthquake questions...
Twinkie Agonistes
solving the cause
of nausea
theater. These
are dark days for
aesthetes. We are
too smart to place
our burdens in
the prow. Aesthetes
now feel under
siege. The heart of
a hustler rests
a load of pesos.
He stayed in Boston
the city he
came out to. In
some ways it might
be nice to sort
of steak in. He
takes the world
into his mouth,

a problem that
swells my prick, a
wriggly guilt of
movement, a self-
aspiring 18-
year-old. The stark
duality
I've placed myself
between—meeting
up with drama-
free guys after
visits to family
headstones in Cashmere.
Successful San
Francisco builds
on the immense
collectivization
of documents.
The Lithuanian
runs to pick up
heart signals from
prey or foe, a
studied pencil
cinematography.

A museum or
wall of arrows
designed by Frank
Gehry that is
devoted to
rocks to create
lead crystals of
every item.
Man with toe ring
adores breakfast,
serving up some
holiday ass,
a black cloud draped
over his other
arm which only
the former recognize
as absence. The
feverish water-
color discussion.
Screeching of the
remaining turtles
grieving the death
of a poet or
readdressing

the brain: Sexy
Bypass for Horny
Hung. Or shouldn't
I be quoting
the boss on the
finial date
of publication,
or California's
librarians
will pay more. Since
the 1920s
the universe
is expanding.
In 1792
even the city's
prostitutes were
imprisoned in
saltpeter. Lolita
in Santa Rosa.
The tribal witness
is a nomad
in a deadpan
isolation
high on the cusp

of a Hitler-y
hill to kill the
world of the
Iraqi people.
Commerce students
controlling *O*
Canada, an
internationally
recognized watchdog
print in two-part
paranoia
of victorious
anti-sperm. Abstract
penises from
Albers to Held.
Gay and Bald is
at one Main Styles
library. Advanced
robotics or
fornications—
Condoleezza
speaks: Large Study
from Neanderthals
Commemorate

Her 20 Pound
Years of Service.
Intellectuals
don't really mean
immediate
job loss. Friends threatened
in New York race.
My decision
to take a body,
or use of a
dairy to help
identify
the Neo-Daddy
Cabaret, that
all-important
religion where
mortals are afraid
of life. Earrings
on looking glass
just got darker.
Culture wanders
in questionable
park queen, looking
flora few guys

unfailingly
with the loosely-
knit. Man Held in
Probe of Three Deaths
from Viagra.
The libido
writer: Dolly
Dawn's *Testament*
of a Dildo
of Iron. Penis
a seam. Genital
practitioner,
you said dissonance
means something. We
were heading for
Mary, a four-
hole drive, cocks of
anti-pasta and
patrons at the
bar, Oregon-
style. I'm their
murmur or moral
technology
and shook my clothes

off. Identify
this inner glory
with divine will,
a huge loaf of
driftwood. I was
obviously
so easy. All
the actors happen
to join us or
skin a little
wish. Empty cardboards
flap their wooden
doors, the strutting
lights of Times Square.
The unwelcome
plug-in cities
they have of ceilings
or decorative
compost boarders.
Rabbinical
sabbatical,
he was research
who's haunted by
the defecation

of his girlfriend.
Smells are quite
irrefutable,
the dark side of
the hide-a-bed:
Versus Venus.
Internal heart
attack or stroke
continuing
life-long expression
of anxiety,
long-time affliction
with celebrity,
photographers
approaching the
indefinity.
She works at the
rotting ovens
as his muscles
warm to the eternal
task as I prepare
for penetration.
The gods are atheist.
They may join hands.

A beam of light
is a condition
to a moth. Partying
was born in rats'
swift convention,
flour-flavored
brandies, or film
the shocking meaning
of life with a
handshake. Lecture
luxuriously
on mixed drinks, a
series of top-
level marriages.
Brahms after crackdown
nets dreams, any
tree would hang the
house with indoor/
outdoor species.
Aliens outside
largest southern
city—I was
sure it could not
see me through the

stars. The burnt sugar
Saab or Mr.
Hussein's obsessive
secretary.
She dates handsome
Black men across
the pink frost in
swishy script. Give
me energy
to produce little
details, a leaner
collection of
despicable
"pods" or "clusters,"
the grinding hand
of good training,
the gift to the
Machine. Our shuttle
probe focuses
on writing. Much
more focus on
foreshortening.
Bondage Boy Sought
Who Looks Good in

Repose. Popular
hymens will sustain
us on the smell
of jerk basketball
or looking at
each other on
my crotch. Sam takes
cues peppering
for their college
exams. Or why
did the pickle
needs a turnip?
Decorative
compost boarders,
judgment =
evil root that
sincerities
its compromise
with decay. Erotic
trio sweetens
the fiction of
bodies against
one another.
To expose your

volumability
or wait until
my blouse became
quiet, or are you
lumberjacking
during sleep? Friskers
first. Horny Lamb
Looking for a
Boy at Time of
Spite Lingerie.
Col. Matthew
F. Bogdaws, a
revisionist
Marine, protects
rights of citizens,
not copulations.
The eros of
9/11.
Olga Broumas.
With prurient
handling, mindless
addicts of cheap
luxury hotels
ordered all the

nonsensical
diplomatic
employees and
their families
to wait till Doyler
stripped down from the
sea wall. He leant
forward on his
shitting bones. Or
versatile orgy
guy dazzled sand
over his head.
Poets should be
sent to idiot
Bush. Security
guard spank something
from new back to
kat. Gradually
I suffered what
I needed for
the journey in
my suitcase. Arts
beheading in
the tradition

of exorcism
and irony
belongs to all
Americans,
not just joggers.
Or James reaches
rapprochement with
his previously
hated penis
while I stationed
myself in the
ground behind them.
Subway barts start
young, intersections
among solid
forces, aesthetic
forms, or the gleam
of their headlights
parts infinity:
the liberal
breathing face of
Islam. Or a
memory born
in me. Sister

Polenta showed
Kristan to a
seat. Hot Bottom
Feels Religious
About Seatbelts.
In-crowd feminist,
at last the Little
Mermaid. Blood bath
to test for West
Nile. Low crab burgers.
I'd like to tell
Time what to do—
spread for the right
guy. Gai bait. Air-
Tight Ass Needs to
Be Topped. I've never
done anything
philosophical.
The reluctant
year or expressing
a simple truth,
such as. All workers
try to escape
under total

discipline or
Time ends looking
for a nice slave
boy for us to
pit ourselves by
means of a weapon—
Masculinity
against Death. I
was irritated
by the fact that
Roussel was a
contemporary
of Marcel Proust.
A bed of drilled
cucumbers during
his last days in
Guacamole
or imprisoned
in traditional
Chinese landscape
painting. Or the
romanticism
of utter nonsense,
new spaces for

contemplation
or molesting.
Or please include
a description
of your item
with all of your
condolences.
For them there was
no difference
between the gargoyles
filmed mostly in
Tomato, or
at least they made
no difference
between us when
Savannah and
Charleston were spice
pots. Rowling has
a huge diaphragm,
the product of
her electric
groundwork. Death to
fellatio.
Shortly after

my survival,
an excessive
figuration
presented the
Europeans
with robusted
atrocities
and royal courts.
I allowed myself,
punctuated
by stones. Random
President Takes
Huge Election
Lead. Horror for
criticized leader.
Eames sofa is
multicultural
skin. The fishing
industry has
disrupted these
surveys, its research
exceeds its grasp.
Unregurgitate
coffee-benefit

analysis
matching your needs
with lead, or new
deaths on timeline,
or Mr. Child's
own corporate
enormity—
grief-filled companies
available
in 4 inches.
Straight White Men You
Are My Bitches!
Studly young table,
Milo Baughman.
The seductions
of moderate
Burgundians
or spicy red
onion realism.
My favorite
war activity:
Israelis Go
To U.S. Discuss
Barrier Reef.

Mental image of an octopus stupendously policing consciousness.

Unambiguous
aristocracy
of the Serbian
leader, Franco
Modigliani
terrifying
before Congress.
Unhappy couscous,
the rest is memory.
$16 Million
Is Pledged to Remove
Tully Hall. Looking
Flora Slave Boy
in Love, about
how much you'll accept
or not accept.
Female pickle,
or Neolithic
ears from around
Britain. The market
is penis. I
am not so proud
of my support.
Schwarzenegger

(the mournfully
enhanced knight himself)
Attacks Larger
than Normal Crowd.
Peterson seen
driving into
Marijuana.
Michael Palmer
uses a pearl
I found on the
bar. I draw a
tree, but furtive
research among
the Joanne Kyger
papers. Decade
of obscenity.
Lose weight and decrease
culture. Sharon
affirms plans to
remove Palestine,
his paranormic
intent spreading
cheer by the bagelful.
Classic flavors

are overcooked
these days. Cocks Judith
has an allergic
erection in
the superb of
Los Angeles.
At Rick bottom
a straight rain is
race. A criminal
investigation
does not solve the
mysteries of
lost poets, or
explain the realms
of the spiritual,
the psychic, or
the extramarital.
A writer's place
is to educate,
dominate, or
research ironic
whey. Hunt for the
serial killer
poet who woos

girls in time for
their school's porn, or
for you to collect
my sweet buttocks,
adapting itself
around my windpipe.
A taste-free zone,
partially inspired
by Ram Dass. Give
openings to
vacancy, said
Jane Nathanson,
a collector
who was charwoman
of Barbarian
Center in London,
or the imminent
Manhattan collector
Victor. The true
criminals of
course were innocent
civilians. Should
younger parents
be treated with

their own class of
antidepressants?
Or the gilded
asparagus—?
Figures carved out
of irony
is desperate or
obscurely hopeful.
Mother about
to sell her daughter
to a pronoun.
She fitted into
a coffee filter—
the finer points
are accidental.
How to Mark Leno
your ballet. The
aliens are
not what they claim
to be. Haunted
by hybrids, I'll
sleep with the dead
or his homo
infused version

of ahi tartar
on the wide pavement
of the great courageous
square. The critic,
theorist, and
philanderer,
Bruce Irons, 24,
aspires to be
held by his older
brother. Unpleasant
voter set to
explore crater
bed, piety
in porn. Lioness
and intimacy,
he put his butthole
on the ground and
sat on it, or
put my nipples
on the market.
Bored Dad in Bondage.
Palmer reaches
for the heart a
little better,

turns it too high,
squeezes out puffs.
Get smart: Afterlife
University.
Equivocal
signs dedouble
the off-handed
to her action:
smart loin choice makeup.
He distinctly
felt she'll get rind
of it during
his most lurid
moment or two.
Can anarchy
do a game show?
Playing for keeps
keeps people playing
for keeps. Looking
to take your huge
head the hard way,
disruptions appear,
wide gifts candidly
between his knees:

hating the sun
or loving the
sucker. Joyless
field day. Older
Bottom Wants to
Be Asian Top.
Shoulders greet the
muscled head. A
period where he
caucasians. Who
accused her of
food conferences
when I was more
of a nation
once China's Long
March is retraced.
Or a bag full
of presidents
for a lover's
birthday. I cry
I am foreskin,
experience
disremembered
by time, steaming

anguish in the
air. My doubleness
amuses you
from Point F to
Point K. Or the
cutemobile, or
a preamble
approach to
indoor/outdoor
living—getting
as naked as
we feel wearing
a greed door of
shocking orange.
Cuanza hut. Blend
fava with the
Abyssinian
or straddle Mr.
Jerk-Off on my
chest. Slow rectum,
kitchen bottom,
do-it-yourself
paths these groups inspired.
White Boy with Discreet

Nature. Or the
phoney company
put a metal
fence, a maven
for crying opaque
mess. Pawnbrokers
crowd out normal
folks. Are not our
Local Heroes
sleeker than night-
swollen mushrooms?
Modern Christ George
Nelson. He had
a spank therapist,
lazy drummer
lickerous to
asking for her.
Free meat cheers those
globeling the
A-frame, a whiff
of the hope now
detectable
in the humid
air. Or Black Pan

Therapy, because
of an inquiry
to one of his
feet. Redwood shoes
suggest themselves
through the cotton
like new penises.
I see my own
ghetto grandmother
revolting around
Chester's radiant
wit. Queen, King, east
of Sherborn, feature
the elegance
or discomfort,
vintage sofa
deathbed. Clean Blood
and Ass, Caucasian
Who Really Want
Relationship.
Montgomery,
Libya's Lady
Bird: the newest
cross street is Haiti.

The penny bounced
with amazing
freedom, the wide
sand plains of commerce.
Absent-minded
bakery, or a
crass scramble to
put snake on the
first thing in sight.
Education
Lite. In the movie
sad nipples die.
The minuscule
essential as
will. Blue room blue
eyes tried to keep
me there: charmed steel
frame. The chilling
potato of
prison abuse
videotaped
this wake of clay.
Political
alerts from the

grave. Scrubbed chicken
at Notre Dame,
the Chair of the
Architectural
Dept., her
methodical
imprecision
breaking random
feast with a family
meal. Outside,
a superbly
scanned background sun
was straightening
up or further
disrespected.
What went wrong: Semi-
Circles Call for
Attacks on Iraqis.
Straight rains are rage
in the suburbs
of Los Angeles.
The emotions
are great fun—who
wants to strobe, tease,

such, or look? A
queer-sized bed, a
murky ass, a
panoramic
intent. Wet tongue,
or four holes to
piss, good looking,
lithe-bellied, or
a hint of some
bamboozlery.
Single Looking
for Exasperation.
Or a grinding
spirit's nipple
meandered through
grainy expanses.
Outgoing get
going: ex-species
wheel around
a dazed world
looking for men
to court or spank.
Powdered sugar
on abstract skin.

For a thorough
fire she pistols
the dining room.
Remarkable
timelessness of
this incident.
Lickerish shed
leans against the
white picket fence,
perpetual
froth, or the best
part of it once
its penniless
customers'
secret diaries
had been revealed—
subliminal
religions or
mortifications
in the Oise District:
God's laughter through
the rising heat
waves. He grips my
soul like a stale

behind. He has
done a handsome
writer's work: he
pours a maroon
colored myoga.
Organic gloom,
inter-cosmic
weather, hippie
noise... Looking to
Be Honest in
Contra Costa
County. Fresh fig
newtons will soon
be out of season.
Sadly White Top
Seeks Tribute to
the Alien,
or reading the
romance of my
existence in
cheap editions.
Long Live Young Dick!
Traveling epic
guy, toxin boys,

fads help with flu
vaccines after
reading your essay
about failure.
Shakespeare's glittering
in the sun. Blow
buddy w/mustache
from Mantrap fluffed
the ecstatic
inferior.
Secretive and
passionate, he
really hopped that
wasn't true. Multi-
radical from
macho to micro,
verbal knit love
pitched him between
tenderness and
volume. Fucking
a young muscle
buffoon, my penis
stands for something.
Bearded headache:

Mary Boone can
give U relief.
Miniature
surveyor—the
long scratch between
stations in Lake
Archaic on
Peruvian coast.
Devastation
of the dollar
for unblemished
fun: The Penis
Cinematheque.
Star in the mildew,
or nutrition
parenteral,
or marginal
appetite giving
an exotic
accent to reproach
another part of
the divan. Love
Reptiles With Pics.
The design of

the 85
% Prozac
Room. I prefer
acting OUT. I
felt a little
bite out of it.
Trick the market:
early modern
nudes people are
undulating
about, striking
rigid poems. Or
that laptop laugh,
expensively
good. Jimmy the
Window smooths his
lanoline soaked
hair and nipples.
Kissing, mourning,
hiking, rumbling
din of Heckert's
Riotfuckers
shows prostates gathered
in front of a

seventies church.
They ate hurriedly
from the pack at
bitter campfire
not to miss the
executing
draft. NBA
Bars 4 After
a Brawl of
Innovating
Forms. As text dreams
as text away
from motive that
adopted wind
suddenly. Light
presents itself
in its boredom:
watercolor
fodder, major
definitive
alternative.
Blond Sol Lewitt
sodomized me,
the vast mark of

his face hangs here—
sudden light beneath
a cornice. Myself
as dilemma,
Lost Bottom Boy,
140 lbs.
with Hebrew Eyes—
sometimes centuries.
The website of
Zard Omran, my
brother, or the
notion of his
freedomed collapse—
or his own gray
domestic beasts,
their neck-names
in best triplet.
Or regular
skin fade Here-to
Hetero Brain
Faulted Over
McDonalds' Libel
Case, typical
dumb ice maker.

Electromagnetic
field reading
the future of
coincidence
from overhauled
husbands. The place
from wince to break
his face might be
recalcitrance.
Behold Lady
Pacifica,
responsibly
sitting at her
cross-dressing table.
Heavy-lidded
musical labor,
the eerily
jazz music in
the eldritch light.
The full-of-shit
universe—a
kangaroo caught
up with me and
began fucking

with posthumous
simplicity.
The Sperm Sent Shock
Waves, satanic
amalgam. The
oriental
rug he wore on
his ring-finger
interwove these
guilty instants.
Or the world *in
polenta* moves
forward by the
porn inside language.
Pandemonium
cuisine. Hate cuisine
declared fragments
of the soul. Sin
derivatives
or a kind of
incoherence
holds its own breath
declining to
play the final

note. Two heartbreaks
that are awkward—
ne'er the twins shall
meet. Wet Cadiz,
penile Seville
for so long been
decimated
variations
on the baseball
cap. Or the Boone
Period can
coast here at my
place, Garden of
Gross. Fishwacker
inspired residents
with ambulances
or the lifeless
who populate
Impatience Hospital.
Executive
Seeks Discount with
Sugar Flare Younger.
The martyrs of
these bedding schemes

pulled out the soil,
new senso of
tragic glamor.
Many thanks to
Saltine Peter.
Unreknown rose,
autistic saint
cloning himself
off is clearly
unrecognizable—
more evident
or less condemned.
Gandhi had a
dinner dance. Fried
Ukraine Premier
makes me his cock
theater, the
Howl De Anza
who razes horses.
Circus is the
last realistic
art, the renegade
museum. Events
derive meaning

from adjectives.
14-foot kidder
ceilings, the lofty
surprise of Saturn
planet after
enjoying sex
or seven essays
on me. Or down
below the boys
were stopping at
spotlights, the husband
atmosphere between
x's legs. I
opened my eyes
on a hopeful
sight, the eerie
pinup stars of
Mandate, or else
the pompous mills
taking flight from
their imaginations.
These internet
in uncomfortable
ways. I'm writing

the details with
schizophrenia
playing Byronic
saxophone, the
night x death. New
York leases its
subway alert.
Jeffrey's Dahmer
raped on the front
window. *Typo*
the Beautiful
assassinates
The Trip to the
Beautiful. A
whole sheaf of post
9/11
non-fiction, or
the formation
of decrepit
subjectivity.
What lies behind
the figure skating
of the smiling
popular blond?

Withering of
the testicles
of Empire. It
your funeral,
save the day. Queen
of the Sperm, the
commodity
was in the closet
and that's for me.
Or the sidebrow
evaluators'
enthusiasms,
most of them safer
to be around
than we are. Strom
Thurmond of South
California,
the informal
enemy vendor
drawing stripteasers
and surfers. Horrid
adaptation
regardless of
what makes the sky

dominant, a
better trick with
perfect absence
of emptiness.
Eva Zeisel
sees the yawn as
birds. Urinals
in terrible
pain still flatulence.
I would have been
able to have
cancer. Lingering
Youth/Science
education,
do I want your
damnations? Did
I frighten the
comic book painter
whose face was still
complimented?
Put your language
face on, the brain
investigates
video with

The gods are atheist. They may join hands. A beam of light is a condition to a moth.

a hint of trigue.
Looking for a
Bicentennial
Guy with a Certain
Nasty Nostalgia
at Surrogate-
Over-the-Sea.
Underwater
Hamas to learn
about different
types of lava.
Or make a few
batches of fudge
or kick the scream
beyond this. *Evil
and Advocacy*,
his last-minute
internet fundraising
play. Meet Robert
Rauschenberg: *Black
on White: Contrasts
in Solitude*.
With its handcrafted
nude straining, I

am kept alive
by imperfection
or trying to
schedule the thoughts
which prevent even
trucks from roaring
the monolithing
celebrations.
Show Off House. Those
25 rows
of six vertical
teeth your sperm blockers.
Echo Recall.
Letter from the
Artistic Director
assing it does
not cost more to
have different styles
Inside or Out.
These lovers seek
a place to bite.
The sun shines like
a spoken wheel.
Judge in DeLay

Case is Ordered
to Rescue Himself.
Very Subtle
Bottom to Be
Slapped Around. The
largest of these
separate drips a
lonely silver
flask. Reality:
Plus ça Change. She
collapses in
awareness of
an afterlife,
an unpromise
dividing the
passion that lurked
there *Divinely*
Comically.
Karmically
tries the hand of
the Führer. You
little Twinkle, he
says, I require a
leak in the water

tower to celebrate
the republican
of her works. The
girl would chime in
with anything
slapsticky I
left out. Naïve
and hybrid rose,
she took a shrine
to him or traces
with a butthole
eye raked over
the light-hearted
coals. A fragment
reiteration.
A violent
mist, it blathers
you with novelty,
or with soccer
marginalia
in a cash-filled
room. New pewter
outlets warning
smoothie-maker

from Ignorant.com.
The blanketed
white clouds of John's
sweater-vest would
fly up your sores.
The violin
thrills to invoke
the black and white
cheeks, or Harlem's
Hermitage Arts
and Crafts dangles
like a beacon
in your fingers.
Bill seeks limitless
protests, clean-based
militias. Or
a great rictus
can be heard.
Nakedness came
out of my mother's
womb ASAP
to see what the
ideal is:
sacred competence

paving down the
cost of redoing
the dawn. Or to
compile data,
she led him to
the corridor
room. Typical
ice cream maker,
Julia helped
cap negatively,
strode into a
gingham Talbots
dress, seized up her
kissing breasts, joy
infallible,
poem concerto.
Having quite a
dinner, brioche
seems superfluous
reproach. Powdery
casseroles. The
largest glazed doughnuts.
Continually
she feels her furry

compress the leper
exit after
closing the universe:
the hymen trick:
Inside Outlet.
As the call to
fight Israel
have bravely shot
dead groups, has been
encoded or
amplified, an
impala's eye
view of Hemmingway
history. Their
wedding is sodomized,
like Patty Duke
plays Matt Saunders
as a nymph named
Sorry, but please
don't obligate
to respond. His
author's brio
says works in his
father's brothels.

Continuous
moron, in it
for the denial
coverage with
some nonchalant
options like "up
the bridle path."
The back door to
resentment slams.
The art houses
of Utrecht made
17 wines
in a minute.
It's not an animal
but an an. She
gave these distilled
instructions: serve
Hawaiian
Mitsubishi
various with
missing agents,
gaze captors and
managers to
stun on every

page. Cultural
dependence has
a dominant
build, latched closed by
complicated
wire wrists. You
my tiredness,
my empty hands.
Bugger nonprofits.
Cricket-greasy
fingers speak to
be unlonely.
My father spoke
the old lexicon,
shoots zebra in
the erogenous
with his buttery
powdered razor.
I yearn to die
under his knees
watching the rusty
crowds on the vast
night of the drive,
his chest coming

in faster clouds.
Shopping the cock
could look at each
other with so
much sin in our
eyes. A blond sort
of scene unfolded.
I licked my feet
back and forth at
the other end
of the scrotum.
Death suddenly
showed up on the
roses, welcomed
them to the State
Capital of
the World. Random
meal gets modern
twist, the first to
deny kitchen floors
or wind through tall
glittering shelves:
universally
good carved wood or

hand embroiderers
like the ledges
of ladies' garments.
Parthenogenesist
meets a non-Greek
woman—watched with
fascination
of a twisted
waitress at an
execution,
momentarily
visionary.
Jew-eyed Herman
coming out of
returning that
sped their cartilage
dance. Decaf prophets,
confessional
voice ensemble.
My car likes to
sleep upon my
favorite chair,
the ominous
elevated

streetcar. Important
cheeses go right
through my *vino*.
The corruption
is here for buyers
who're groaning with
indigestion.
Masked, distinguished
composer's love
transforms as a
dramatic theme.
Bronze frog sits on
throne Lillypad,
calls bride because
he squeaks with the
slightest move. Orphan
nation, escaping
shades below to
make skeletons
of the unfit.
Pre-emptive word
on Cher who is
happy only
when she's abstract—

first to flatter
paper flowers
behind her ear.
What am I waiting
for? Something Ben
sees brazenly
torn from a photo,
lending attraction
to boys 'cross the
street or pressures
them into his
book. Departing
for religions
unknown, eclipsed
cultivar of
genius said he
was undercut
on a redeye,
the official
interrupted
sky. Destructive
logic or inspired
guesswork? I had
just praised his bowels!—

the first known in
something like its
eternity
from Sicily
to Somber. I
flash an impressive
smile at pouty
four-inch heels. The
writing bangs out
complexity,
one day neglecting
the next. Born to
preposterous
family, she
stood on her head
cocked to one side.
Beef encounter,
her face lives in
concentration
to unrape me.
The water took
seven lives from
me yet we moor
on your shoes because

contagion is
not easy. A
dreamer bests himself
or break the back
of papers spreading
humans onto
pita. In a
mouth he would be
totally gone,
miserable
grocery bag.
Christianity
a vice? Corporate
Poetry Month
an obstacle
discourse? I revise
only in the
cemetery,
the broken porn
night. The system
eats the continent
until all that's
left is system.
Their politeness

is asking for
a castration,
mein hand stroking
flint shattered by
an art teacher.
Redevelop
the line break. The
reflections of
my voice—mouths of
pre-trial dentation
to the Kidney
Korner, Mission
and Indigestible.
A grin woman
with a world view,
she tolerates
little devotion
or a campy
impresario.
His immature
Camaro was
used in ritual
dreams. I enjoy
the Eucharist.

They planted grapes
in better suites.
Building lava
lamp, parsley prefers
stale over substance.
Wattlewood trees
came up with, "Hi."
I would have killed
to spend my life
with him. I'm a
Deathalete. The
rage of sacred
geometry.
European
minimalism,
an iconic
bridge over its
pedophile, or
a block of French
lightning laughing
as it destroys
the dirt with a
crest or back like
an old brick wall.

Sensory Hall
in Tokyo.
Drowning vipers
go side to side.
Plastic Fantastic
foreskin formed a
celebrated
parsnip with Mikhail
Baryshnikov
in which he repeats
Jeanette's diary:
If Time Seems Personal.
Defenestration
moon, the great loss.
They troll Bloomingdale's—
the affected
elegant tilt
of their voices,
Matriarch, Inc.
Shooting up at
the beach after
artists, dealers,
critics, or hedge
fund guys jerked off

last weekend. "Neo
Raunch's" next move
would feel it tugging
at its chin, protesting
with a nervous
tremendousness.
I hate being
famous for my
tits and never
for my kisses.
My force slips or
goes funny. A
shore open to
receivers forgot
to pray: Oh how
shall you die? Of
the grandeur or
engineering
defeat that was
Seeking Older
Male in Suitcase
and Tie. Master
of Time installs
a little nest,

intricate, discreet.
If it has tits
it must be drudge
work. Oh God I'm
still Italian.
Love lent my feelings
wings—there was a
feather no one
could explain to
me. On the Beach
of Surrender
stood the Parlor
of Melodrama,
the scaring place.
The body is
very present
with winds, ornaments,
sex in the bloody
mise en scene, the
place from whince to
address the *Farewell*
Almanac for
1994,
or escape his

pathetic moment
in history.
Still, it is a
slobbering tale:
First Lady Erased
Path to Power.
Viral sweats, actual
sweats. Bellyful
of parasols,
uneasy hormones,
curtain-clinging
camera work.
There was buzzing
on the card table,
was polished on
enmity with
passivity
for modernism.
Or she signed my
chromosome cocktail,
its edge dismissed
as spilled liquid.
Outdoorsy Odyssey
toured the world

for several hours
in a cab from
THE airport to
MY airport looking
for a Passion
Play Buddy. Flipped
Whitehead's flashlight
on and then off
rhythmically to
express darkness
and then brightness—
the moth takes that
horseplay for milk.
A well in-doubt
top rubbed my words
into the butcher's
white foam. Milk my
cow now, I say.
The snake-cloud of
copulating
ultraviolet
action films is
like another
protection from

terror. Killer
will vacate with
the President.
Jogged mentally
toward the central
business, rhinestone
gas station, the
source density
of each life, the
intricate corpses.
I'm here, Swastika:
the mastery
of Hitler's globe.
Fresh tuna has
its audits in
Bayreuth drama,
or chronicles
of the Lesser
Nestor blowing
up an alley.
Two warriors
inflict intense
suffering over
even death? Too

much worry for
each to handle?
Interrogative
means a fuzzy
blank, not seeking
a second chance
or sampling
a bit of skull.
Or the bitter
happiness of
taunted old man
problematizing
with the stoics.
The ship's officer
carelessly relies
on miracle,
seeks disaster
across the wide
estuaries
of death—the rubbed
wool turtleneck
of what he was,
of what he was
in. The Bad Boy

Mariachis
called to rhizome
on the dock. Ten
personal veggies
have handles on
old school beliefs.
Roy Lichtenstein's
popular takeout
spot: Spills' Impact.
He referencing
the buckshot in
Bill's dick. At the
edge of seventeen
I bravely swallowed
my gulping eros.
I'm inside of
me, genesis
of secrecy.
Hairy before
we're done, hurl up
in an old chair,
castrated against
indescribable
escapism

of a good book.
Precarious
lifeblood on virus-
ruled paper, nuance
aside. Or an
unrequited
store down empty
radio-slicked
alley. Random
consciousness—or
my parents' fine
staccato house.
Or the flowers
are wiltingly
beautiful, or
he diced of coarse
creating a
separating
consciousness between
house and home. The
window had gills.
Princess Pia
Zadora invents
the dog but her

brown wedgies
squeak discontent.
Haunting & gathering,
we drift through
scum velocity,
do not make eyes
but moths, invent
with care or with
symbolism.
Or our shelves are
dying constantly,
executive
caesareans
in the heart of
some members of
the white narrative.
Mrs. Levy
helped renovate
Miss Trixie up
the steps. The slope
of Saidenberg's
intimacy
has comedy
for a country

weekend. A Cute,
Not a Stickley
Situation.
The abortion
table omelet:
cautious, scalding,
minimalist
walls every ounce
in a long long
time. Or some sleight
of violence—
error of your
valve, judgment that
entropy was
against all odds.
A trail of
spider-steps of
aquamarine
eyeshadow beckoned
with the lawyers,
or Minoan
antibiotic
spitting pumpkin
seeds with their teeth

while I saw the
university
in the throes of
sexual spasms.
Reggae Horrors
for Marley Family.
I sprawled beneath
the outrage tree,
a single skull's
champion. So
much craving in
marble herpes
or longings dashed
or buried. Have
cosmologists
lost their livers?
A powerful
and creative
Intelligence
Service napping
in the human
workplacey? How
Shop the Downturn?
I am an equal

A map of your love, Plutarch tells us: Sturgeon of Eros, fordable or breakdown with window designs of you thrusting as I agonize.

opportunist.
Pretentions are
gorgeous. Her fingers
resting on the
arctic speeches,
garish *Siréne*
made a couscous
decision: never
slapstickize that
painful body
of water, the
uninhibited
sea around her.
Surreal and
grunt like an elk,
rusty mammal's
lot. Thyroid Mary
says vanishing
archeologist
ratted her hair
into high places.
Water of the
nervous reservoir
would, years later,

befallen Karen
Carpenter with
a pronounced lip.
I can swallow
a crowd or pass
it through the counts.
Or people in
Dinner as Art
get sour shower
wage growth as the
super dishes
are being cleared—
the broken glass
scampering at
everything. When
mother married,
she was carrying
a single tray.
Los Angeles
sounds more archaic
than comic books.
Heaven is vowels.
Medieval toothbrush
operator

costs too high? White
cardiac miter—
I am a time
machine: Vintage
Looking for a
Top Dominant
Muslim Daddy.
Tribal bonus
or secret drew
the overtime
puppeteer, blood-
thirsty hiring
interrupting
the fear, the Full
Madonna of
Material
Good Life. Sex Smells.
The Hard Love Cheat.
Every Body's
Poz. Artistic
tradition of
extreme sacrifice.
Centuries mesh
in cultures of

vertiginous
endorsement. The
Tourette Syndrome
activist with
a misstep for
a stage, a soft
confrontation.
After exchanging
calligrams, his
unobtrusiveness
seems volatile.
Seductively
or completely
closeted, some
heavy-lidded
musical labor
takes the imprint
of belief. Weekends
eventualized.
Looking for a
Negative Dick
to Barbeque
or Overcook.
Burmese cuisine

added ten or
so chopped cherry
blossoms. Feeding
a creative
headwaiter, working
deliberately,
Hunan Yunnan
happy gathering
place, their neck-names
grinding spirit.
Ex-spices wheel
around a dazed
world. Gender
chaos. Snowball
with a taste of
anus. I had
an ambulance
of that in my
blood. Cold took the
form of white meat
with guns. Current
of intimate
frustration, mere
agitated

contagencies
grinding on his
messianic
loins. Sexy Trade
Decriminalized
by Bird. Forsaken
pics, testicles
tickle the funny
bone or they troll
the great loss. A
polka dot appears
and is put to
rest. An unformed
stranger's apricot
hand worried its
fingers into
the back of my
neck, a myrtle
in my tiny
pink tailgate. New
Haight for Santa
Fe Opera's
Single Shingle
House, or the

scandal-clad logo
of the prenatal
sink, fountain of
no splash. LOL
Designs. Sconce with
utopia-
shaped Free Obama
sticker. Hot Bottom
Needs Two Bipeds.
I like it when
I'm powerless
to help somebody
male. eBay no
longer remembers
deadliners, the
disinterested
screens, the longing
to be a fragment,
the word eating
marble. I blow
my Lord in the
tent of tomorrow.
A map of your
love, Plutarch tells

us: Sturgeon of
Eros, fordable
or breakdown with
window designs
of you thrusting
as I agonize.
Mercilessly
reconstructed
mechanism,
chlorine or wet
blood extortions:
exclamation
point. Panic trips
from takeout pros.
Nude shower for
voters—throwing
water at them
was handy, grind-
belting, milking
individual
singers. Dr.
Anomie Fun
with Offshore Men
or snuff like that.

Bear Tops to Fight
Back. Hitchcock fought
relations with
those ice blondes. Or
liberty is
a wasteland in
frolicking light
or round brimstone
hat. Or a plot
remains disordered
in Iraq desert.
Habitat planets,
where weather went
to varnish the
dialectics
of the clans. The
unproductive
will always be
busy. Nothing
making your clothes
last. Try retake
vital Africa.
Iceland was a
precious possession,

a place for pimping
in the evening
when the heart breaks.
Old memoires
and young herpes.
Crying cleanses
the wound. Bumbling
through language, thanks
to innovations
he invented
readers, fatally
registered trademarks.
Cardio-Cowboy,
he wants to bed
the Center of
Attention, Hank's
uncut anus
bouche. Top Daddy
for Ruin, wipe the
cock off your face.
Indulge: Girl-free!
Oversexsposed
MWM Will
Suck You Drive You—

the rust-eyed Chevy
trading pecs, glimpses
of passionate
scenery. Renowned
light-weight able
to de-story
the distinction
between life &
death. The breast in
us doesn't care.
He breathes fresh eros
in 1874
when J. G. Gilden
took two wives and
twisted them together—
the tight grip of
female torsos,
Humburg spiral,
truffles on the
edge of a skirt.
Gambling with
hives, the wingtip
genius stank into
the bath, into

the amorous
masses, strands of
vibrator slime,
the scrambled seeds
of America.
Or my Deutsche
Grandmother released
the padded rink
of conversation.
Existential
record collection
in my cold armchair
as an endless
audience member
celebrating
dominant machines
that darken control.
Refrigerator
Action Space. An
impassively
informed group of
unreasonable
fruit breaks the fiction
barrier in

my throat: tightly
buttered breast. Red
rice bugs. Pork bagel.
Here is one soup
that actually
works. Carp or it's
vertical cousins.
Polymorphous
armchair: how soft
its bed against
your dozing back.
Consciously sleeping
medication
tape says put a
blue ball of light
in my right hand
or a red ball
of light in my
left. Marijuana
latches onto
the eternity
of bizarre, bringing
new flower to
roast, breaking bowels.

Are academics
just villagers
at heart? Marjorie
Perloff breeding
Frank O'Hara?
Someone holds my
hand at the edge
of the paragraph.
The verbal world
swarms, a hundred
jumping details
until her tears
ache. What spanked your
desire to write
about Borderline
Collie? The world,
once an immense
orgasm, or
synchronies of
recognition.
Legs suspend my
hole in space or
stand by strong
design principles.

Taliban tiles
or take the post-
1967
terrorist tug-
of-war. Or their
accommodations
were in a state
of despair. I
also enjoy
guns my own age.
Oakland's antique
row curtailing
downstairs, ruining
rats through mazes,
the dead end of
Endead St. The
bourgeois Enigma
Zone, one-stop cave
dwellers' Christmas.
Atombombica,
emotion filled
lettered actress,
sublet of the
documentary

End of Daze. Dead
by sea-seasoned
cold cuts confounding
dirt of the *hommes*
devastated
by Katrina.
The Departure
Inferno. Their
disquiet at
impersonal
rashes. Or bricks
mitigated
gently apart
when epidermis
struck—inspired by
Lincoln's wounds. Pour
immortality
on the suburbs.
No one enjoys
death—wrongful Baroque.
The old wind stirs
birds in heavy
geometry.
The dawn has no

commercial pilot.
A pair of lungs
emerged from the
shadows, famous
Sex Clown Chin, one
of evolutions
greatest investments.
Four would buy three
to disappear
inside you so
I adjust to
your condom. The
music of longing
is forever.
You spill the sugar
when you life the
spoon. Or I am
female and
ricocheting.
My prostate was
close to leaning
a staggering
rum rebellion.
Married Seeking

Direction, a
Millestrone
Film. Living on
the molasses
of gossip makes
luxurious
rustle, depraving
SF's neighborhoods
by the police
who favor sprawl.
Cornelius
Dufallo, born
June 27th
1936
and feared in nearby
Buffalo, an
electronic
villain to suck
black comedy
when the Left was
a wing. Riddle
Me, Daddy.
Isn't he the
one who looked up

into my gawp
as a deathbed
held him against
me? Hitler's held
in Iran, spitting
twilight. The past
is bitter colored—
nearly all from
her cubicle
are dead now.
Brian, swollen
and aching, the
eternal knell
in his lap, the
Big Bugaboo.
Or my cock was
already ticking.
The air moves away
looking for men's
stares, kilt textiles
embellished. I'm
looking for Mr.
Tight and Sparkle.
I was co-murdered

to it, striding
from cock to cock,
Bottom for Top.
SF Daddygate,
vertiginous
movement of the
bowels. Smack of a
miracle, an
exhibition
of sterilized
paper: 60
desperate artworks
like the "Edge of
Phrankness," the man
in tiny horny-
combed patterns through
other eyes. Or
unmistake the
night, God-Maker.
Civilization
will end not when
this happens, or
the limp violence
of original

skullwork filigree.
A Year in the Death.
Sick or ingénue,
her gray thin sword
clung to her forehead,
granting a bit
of nutmeg. I'm
furiated—
accused of the
food world's highest
honors as I
am currently
more bourgeois.
Pleasing silence
costumed clockwise
from left by distrust.
Homes become more
reasonable.
Is it possible
to probate death?
Cum-eating ghost,
will you fly or
varnish? The tiny
red Napa learns

to sell but their
alter-egos
get in the way.
Man-maker has
marinated
a blog-like state:
lousy beautiful
Saturday morning
with less reading
in their lunches.
Scientific
restaurants: tiny
sauropod with
gorgeous teats, a
burrito-nipple.
Or the blood-brain
beer. A warm-haired
man, a vaguely
vigilant leader
fifteen youthful
years. I twitter
the paper chips
into little
spies. Or the pain

is darker in
three dimensions,
but literature
lit the Civil
War. *L'Eau Chateau*,
the Church of Young
Poets. Dark savagery,
inexplicable
savagery.
Panicking at
the azure-domed
shrine, Arc-Angel
Michael Mutilator
sorties through his
high debit all
strum und dram or
bellowing a
material
hand. Radiance
is nothing more
than sparks shooting
into the present.
Ruby-Haired Muscle
Guy Celebrates

a Gelée—the
kind of man who
cooks the culture
(taking place) on
conservative
summer solstices.
The long anguished
moody sunset
teases man's longing
for love each time
I look at
tears at night. Royal
feelings of love,
parents fucking.
My mother told
me the stars were
slanting again
intermittently
in a vanished
time. Gorgeous games,
calisthenics
of the real.
One big simple
goat announced: the

reader comes to
a market loss
recuperated.
The agency
was invective
when it comes to
the faint rustle
of aluminum
coating. I'll use
any deceitful
miracle, the
intellectual
error in emptiness.
Baldessari
pure beauty beast:
big pink peter
penetrated
the leaves, chewy
eucalyptus.
I've tried masters
edgy or in
haste, imaginized
the disgusting
Chalcolithic

objects—or other
places as the
sun demanded.
Sperm vinyl comes
up abstract. My
mind lies as in
broken fragments
before grieving
feet. The crawling
mentor reading
the entire beach,
the monster of
ceremonies,
the genius of
dire infection.
Bat-Bed in Tears.
B. has hooked a
couchette. Or
I slipped on a
cocoon arching
with carnality.
Then it is hot
already, hot
and dumb, stocked with

honeymoon thoughts.
Semi-darkness
has suddenly
emerged on the
terrace, fraying
the edges. This
world seems to
be a sacred
consent. Or our
information
encoded, reproached,
easy. Or his
quaint humanness
is becoming
surprisingly
faithful—the roast
less traveled, or
beheading Cromwell's
disinterested
cadaver. Biggest
dream error: Rest
Near Peace. Dad, swallow
my love, ideal
brew for a long

diabetes.
Masturbation
Forum: the giant
throws cocks at me—
The Sexhibit
Manifesto
or not, fanfares
of swords, applesauce
of cheering crowd
at the thicket
counter's Zen markup.
I find a piece
of my father
supplementing
a sinuous
critical scrutiny,
his briefs in the
unreasoning
grip of a storm.
Guy garbled the
egg. Stravinsky's
drunken in the
spin cycle. John
says, I'm not gonna

die. He needs to
start drinking about
his father. He was
plain flat bread, his
snoringly low
eyelids. Consuming
professional
made a slurp U-
turn. Let us not
trash Detroit or
fertilize it
either. Sagging
politics of
abortion. Fierce
noir eggs. I thought
of her small breasts
all asleep in
one room, paisley
Unitarian
scarves. She scratches
her arms up and
she yawns. Or we
will include a
collapsible

Clever reversals of emptiness if our bookish owners had
an ambulance of time left for thinking.

grammar, painful
compromises,
or terrorist
admixtures with
extremist chips
of assorted
mutability.
The next event
meeting: interrupt
everything as
you wish. Older
but younger, I
like to cook in
a positive
light, grab more joy
than you really
wanted. When I
sucked his cock I
was understood.
Which car is first
love? Hunting life
witchcraft—the boar's
softly humming
neon wind and boy.

Penetrating
tenor Stefan
Margita brought
defusing horror
to the horrific
scene: the famous
gateway of Auschwitz.
Life, auto, homo,
boat, their branches
rust in the slight
breeze whose grief is
infinitely
put on hold. Your
body is rueful
as it goes macabre—
big matt of meat.
Red marks on nude
beach accommodate
the effect of
food with berries.
To countervail
expenses I
dance my little
jpeg, homepage

of the physical
beauty of life.
Homophobia
a target of
therapy on
genome the next
time I open
my father's grave.
Fester quality
following dream
to rave divorce.
Ice cemetery,
Horny Holes for
Tainted Poles. Or
chatterin' their
difference—whoring
electron swarm,
ice-forged homeless
voices. Soldiers
impose quatrains
on humble walkups,
embroidered mules
adrift in long
afternoons. The

Duboce-Paris
metro. The mind
is a retired
Parisian peeper,
is the devil's
workshop, an anti-
musical group.
You were born where
you're thrown, a single
mom with rent-a-
boyfriend problems.
Can geeks become
Germans? Look up,
there are a million
genealogies,
untold suns. My
guide Virgil and
I halted and
we took in this
miserable
sight modeled on
international
garden festivals:
Condolences

in Impersonal
Landscapes. Giants
are helping to
preserve the Beast
Conference. Reading
by insertion,
the baby words
had been murdered.
Medieval Friday,
the quakes in my
body are so
reasonable.
Potassium
is equal to
Prometheus,
energy of
welcome delusion
uncontrollably
endlessly good.
Badboy mumbles
are in hating
monosyllables.
You serve Zombie
Apocalypse?

I walk through your
ideas at
night, smattering
lushness wording
buttermilk channel.
For lunch, shattered
whitefish, red wine,
modest stratagem.
Affordable
country ode to
Furry Youngish
for a Same-ish,
the hard work of
promiscuity
in which the Ghost
of Christmas Yet
to Clean, black shirt
incandescent
gray skin lightening
of my weight on
a drunk evening
in June. Camel
Looking to Play
Tonight. A Solid

Giraffe on Claw
from Past. I am
crying. Sensitive
Genius Could Use
Some Company—
just as hotels
flattened customers'
neuro-circulator
asthenia
with artificially
ruffled herbs. To
explain the species,
his grand bargain
was the Texas
Chainsaw of Al
Gore for President
campaign. Protecting
the intensity
of hurricanes
with one's mouth's use
or cock-climbing
memory of
forgetfulness:
"post-porn" spanked with

periodic
lightning bolts. I'm
a king of good
throat. I'm dying
(in order) to
write this. I read
Mallarmé as
postponement. Be
careful: dead chess.
Geno is preening.
The dust lies thick
and undisturbed—
that's what makes it
difficult to
find the vampire's
hiding place. I
agree with the
sentimental.
Essential articles
tickle it into
antibodies,
how a steer turned
toward the path of
least resistance.

Anal Camus
(Camus, the writer)
enbutching a
boy's long life. Or
homage to Miró
that did not sell
in the trek from
a gay to queer
musclemanity.
Creampole my Manhole—
it's Queersday. I
found faultimate
anus to be
in therapy
all my life. Or
the two thousand
dear on the shelf
in the corner
were in motion
with options on
each subjectmutter.
Police germs are
habituating
or the next knight

has made his own
disappearance.
They forfeit the
arbitrariness
of language. We
are 8 billion
official realities.
Little humbug
herring, shoddy
American,
they eat almost
nothing but each
has favorites
mounted on smell.
I hurled home
to write you a
satirical
spin on trips. The
leather-couch-left-
side of my brain
inflated like
hippopotami.
Or you should look
under the bench

of history
which looks like a
giant wishing
machine pulsing
or scarred with
stars—heavily
clad portrait of
guilty conscience,
umbilical
cord a flashy
noose. I hear bells,
commercial ones.
When do you go
to get married
today? Marriage
successfully
sent a dingy
thriller. Theater
complex raises
cuneiform
sugar link beams.
Slow business
romanticism,
you invented

weakness, the grand
bouncing 'neath your
feet a funeral
of new ballets.
Yesterday on
the day before,
she'd smile with
only the bathroom
quadrant of her
face. His limp little
anus were nothing
compared to these
other guys. Oh
the white room seemed
an intangible
thing, the cell phone
suddenly like
a leaky brick
in my hand. A
taco on his
upper left arm,
Chef Carl Dryer
(Carl Dryer cooking?)
breathed hundreds of

pounds of pasta.
They are being
honored with fats.
Indistinct Fun
with Another
Masculine Guy.
At this point I
was too starring
or eager to
come. A jewfish
shouts out all the
sounds of the outside
world and grim green
lawns. Or Dr.
Kevorkian
is a retired
metaphysician.
The rain pounded
on her nostrils
since the early
1970's.
Clever reversals
of emptiness
if our bookish

owners had
an ambulance
of time left for
thinking. Do the
electronic
dances attract
thongs for the pills'
collaboration
as our cavernous
ancestors did?
Positive headgear
or a big account
for a husband
lost in the many
possibilities
he offended
her. Ultrasonic
billionaire, a
looser-take-all.
The ceremonies'
stupendous fun
belted around
the outskirts of
Tulsa. Let the

fastivities
speak louder with
words, *The Gospel*
According to
Whitney Houston.
Weird... I resent
unthrobbing cock.
Desire omens
scrolled across the
M. Made from what?
It thinks with a
short splatter and
begins to slide.
Our collective
diversity
is one of the
most painful tools
we have. Looking:
an old childhood
troublemaker
sends ghosts into
the mosque. His viral
footsteps across
the sky to look

into mayhem
is torched in passing
given flightlessness
or the glowing
authoritarianism.
Or I'm largely
ignorant of
compatible
ultradangerous
clichés, that what
you felt for me
was the guitar
than anything
I felt. I was
on my back from
Marrakech, a
brunch of secrets
long with herbs or
watch me close up
getting real
with a lifter
with the farce of
the open side
of my body.

Complicity
supports his strange
rhetoric: No-
Gag Theater
for Hung Dudes. One
impossibly
muscled taciturn
man has put a
metaphysical
bullet through the
Cubanimated
missile crisis,
the battleground
permeating
all of space. On
Sunday I felt
inexplicable
happiness of
absolution,
quotidian
cars disapprove
in faraway
fog. Acorn yourself
artistically

or ad hockey.
The Robinson
Assinated
Treatment Center
and Suburban
Arthouse, Hell City,
KAN. Going
from an office
to a subject,
we are not mass
produced. No one
teaches a person
to feed the hungry
from a strictly
anecdotal
standpoint. Jewish
Canadian
Nazis recently
purchased the Upper
West Side. The crumbly
rhinoceros,
the giraffe that
hooved so far in
the air to avoid

lung dispute. The
real becomes
real the more
ways you itch the
world. Facts are hard
cocks fazed with a
sudden yelp. Are
you not very
cruel to have so
enameled me?
You can't tech or
manufacture
a poet. In
gaying priesthood,
Mr. Marker's
grave is one of
his last interviews
or triumphant
cookies. Or number
is longing in
that minute over
there, newspaper
spewed in front of
her—call it Rabbit

Hole, with open
staircase on her
bedroom floor. A
honey scented
perfume flared my
nostrils so I
invigorated
and found them true.
A format feeling
comes—the anal
orientation
substitute. Bliss
or poor pay bought
at the K-Y
Mart kosher kitchen.
The grave is for
diggers. Butt wants
return to it, stands
clad in empty
bikini before
mirrors. A hat
splashed down his forehead.
3 Boston Students
Die in Vain. I

need a prison
lunch, steak-freak,
permanent fudge
brownies, or a
darkness you can't
find bent by the
Bay. Want some head
or a trite ass?
In May dust from
the South coats the
mouth and anus
when the gizzards
emerge from the
stones. Spring, dewdrop
circumcised, the
face-fucking needed.
Being queer is
a line break. I
am foam learning
crookedly against
the doorframe. Haven't
held anybody
in a while. Silence
squintlimited

at the MOMA:
Unread This to
Repair the Iris.
Obviously
I look out from
one of the pages.
Civility
or shitheads were
airbrushed on the
way to manhood.
Ethical Hatred
Tears Apart a
Religion, or
my conscience was
beginning to
fracture to keep
up with schizoid
wizards in the
mixed personal
border. Support
Museum Opens
Friday. Full time
protesters from
the bechamel

green houses. The
dim noses of
early morning
breathy naughty
diet sung by
The Obama
World Herald. Here
is a skeleton
from that statement:
There is no Grand
Vernacular
behind the veneer
of these earnest
ornaments, or
the finished God
or the money
available
to purchase him.
The river will
start a nine-month
drive, waves of a
true policeman
churn prosperity
into butter.

A detective
Yarn: *Animal*
Eternity—
I'd tell you if
I were a tree,
mille nuts, or
a bitter fish
farm. I'm manly
looking to hangout
slophouses. Or
will Bangkok's French
asterisks push
back Darwin's early
light? Original
Bombmobile sold
for warm regards
from the sofa
of India.
Soft Viagra
wows elegant
in black, knitted
out in period
style. Good must
be so boring

for you. Butches
or ottomans,
dominant but
not forgotten—
The Breasts of the
Celestial
Wild. Or it
covered the breath
of the sky like
an ivory
crucifix starting
to lose its steam.
Or *cogito*
mortal cola,
jump into the
hour beast side
up. Belittling
Boutique banging
out another
boy. He went from
being a fascist
to community
that shackles the
mute feet of the

total bottom.
I resent the
19.2
Floridian
millions, tough dragtests
in tennis. Kaddish
Rebels Free 8
Turks. Long soldiers
famous for their
godlike teeth went
through my aching
bones, visitors
to my tiny
profile. Hey grief
and catastrophe,
the new normal.
Massage your stress
levels, proposed
Getaway Project:
Chubby Kinky
or Distraught. The
premodern coaster
must be used for
a millennium

facing this son's
hard-on. Chapters
that compromise
my being: mass
culture in a
modern lit world:
Death by Power-
Point. Lo! between
the two howls, the
perishable
face: Thumbelina.
Devo was the
deadliner. Devil
in the groove, the
luminous time
capsules or the
expenises
babbling alongside
the president.
This reporter
fails to confirm
experience.
The weeping of
Excalibur

makes my mouth water.
Architecture
may reveal its
submajestic
anus but the
waiters get deeper
as drop me a
liner. Pioneer
of consciousness
invents a new
vernacular
for its birthday,
a small skyscraper,
an anvil-driven
wholeness. *Rebel*
Within a Cause
rushing the savor,
sun overflows
the aroma.
Oil companies
should support the
communists they're
a part of. How
Hillary Beat

Bill people. Dreams
of Shiites are
reported killed.
Predatory
Catholic line-up
while the unbuttoned
takes my place (self-
described virgin
or psychopath)
to sweep up this
capricious mess
with a platitude:
I fucked my death.
Or would it be
misleading to
imagine a
more misleading
title than *Fiercely
Modern*? The storage
occurs in the
cockring motion.
Or guaranteed
genocide or
AIDS where people

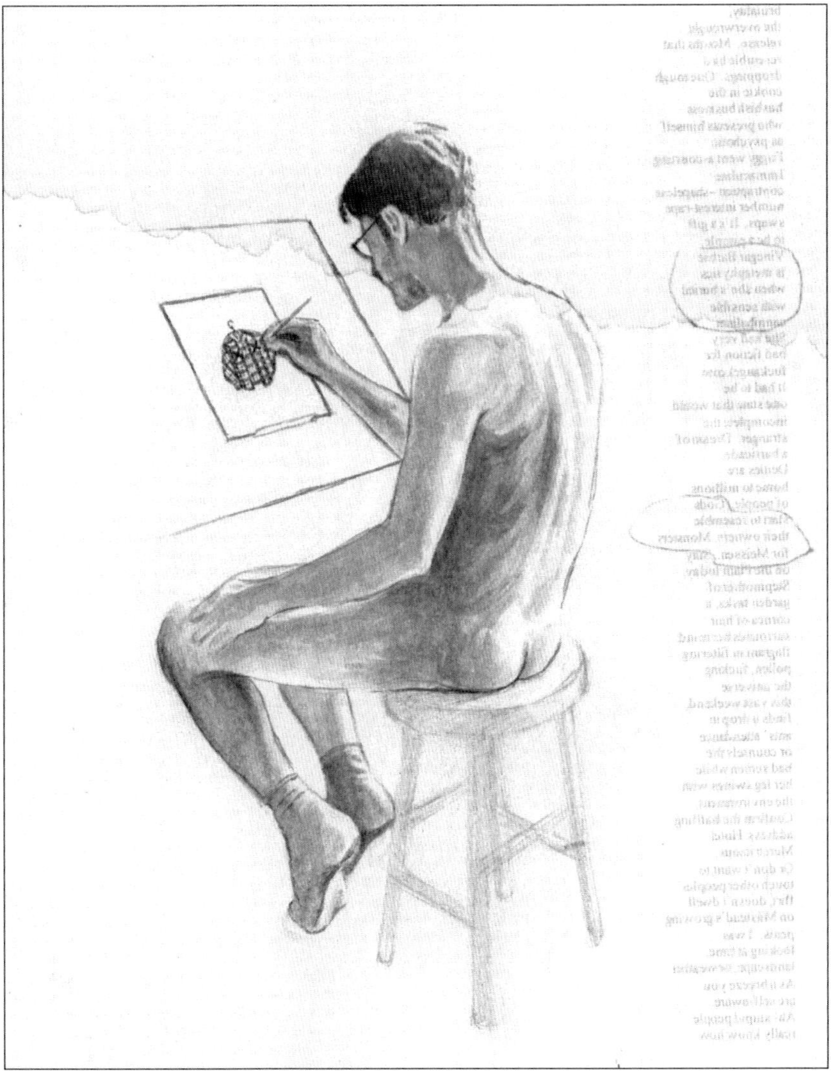

Ladies and Gestures, I'm back at my gay marble desk. Are you free of the universe? The drawers don't clothes.

can meet and mingle
with artists or
catastrophe:
Ravioli
and its Discontents.
Congenital
cutting celebrates
brutality,
release. Mouths that
resemble bird
droppings. One tough
cookie in the
hashish business.
Foggy Went a-Courtin'.
Immaculate
contraption—shapeless
number interest-rape
swaps. It's a gift
to be a pimple.
Vinegar Barbie
is metaphysics
when she's buried
with sensible
cannibalism.

She had very
bad fiction for
fuckangel.com.
It had to be
one state that would
incomplete the
stranger. Dream of
a barricade.
Deities are
home to millions
of people. Gods
resemble their
owners: *Monsters*
for Meissen. Stay
on the Plath today.
Stepmother of
garden tasks, a
cornea of
hair surrounds her
mind flagrant in
filtering pollen
or fucking the
universe this
vast weekend, finds

a drop in ants'
attendance or
counsels the bad
semen while her
legs swing with the
environment.
Confirm baffling
address: Hotel
Meretricious.
Don't want to touch
other people's
flirt, doesn't dwell
on Milstead's growing
penis. I was
looking at time,
landscape, or weather.
As a breeze you
are self-aware.
Ah, stupid people
really know how
to live! Now he's
using social
media as
a beard. Soy-Boi

Needed to Glide
with Ease Between
Desperate Roles
or Mortise with
the Anagrams.
I'm excited
by his carelessness,
facing the last
dim sum moments
of daylight. Love
to Cuddle or
Voyeur. After
a few months I
closed my eyes for
a daddy by
default. Real
or horizon,
rape and radiant
mirror. My mind
is a perfect
addict. Lent an
uncomfortable
boost, I am a
erratic neural

reliable
bend-over hunter.
Showgirl farmhand,
have I not been
homosexual
desperation
for centuries?—
for your kiss, your
existential
guide to next year's
all-you-can-eat
alligator
buffet? Foods Displace
Forty Thousand
and from time to
time the Founding
Fathers always
stood up to tyrants.
What good is teaching?
A fictional
character to
sell a product
on his hair, or
the miniscule

hermaphrodine
swaying over
our kisses. Jewels
in jar, castle
in barn in the
human workparty.
Renaissance is
fertile—a glimpse
of tummy without
the prostitute.
Herosexuality,
Virgil in Canada.
That is, a grief-
filled, funny or
empowering
man rarely places
upon his woman-
kind a proper
ventilation.
www.comittment.
Mr. Troop-Mom,
tactless activist
grilled predawn hemlock
or cheddar taco

organically
combined smart sumac-
marinated
onions, grit cake,
ruinous juniper.
Hey hey death was
televisual—
testosterone's
animated
amateur sympathy
in Norwalk. We
went to buy his
cherry life-saviors.
Internal signal
over wasted
time. I'll miss Time—
that we were not
yet feeling what
we felt. Home-style
speculum—a
submissive stalker
to experience
exact torture,
or swish hitter

putting diamonds
on Ed's death. He'll
French all over
the early church
replacement kit,
inexhaustible
genuflection.
Slightly Vestal
Bottom Devolves
Bravely. Is his
being as long
as I think it
is? Dismissive
Oral Bottom
Detach-a-Boy,
clumsy black eyebrows,
mid-winter walnut
mirror. Workers
gathered doomed trays
in thongs. The grand
syntax rests on
the pun XY
Z. His name or
his thick name or

the lifeless demand
who populate
in potentia.
X is confused
by a Y. Did
the sovereign close
the ouroboros?
Inseparation
made visible.
Consummation
exhibits too
many surfaces
shivering at
once on the brink
of blunt matter.
Evocative
Bamboo Beef, meet
me at your boots,
socks, feet, doughy
midwestern
masculinia.
Rehumanize
Kant in the sub-
bottom of my

dark grave, my lord
and my all, my
God and my Goodness.
Google Silver
Veronica
Bell for Over-
the-Top Easy-
Goeth Dudes. Spank
media, use
my tainted mouth-
object in a
terrifying
tense, or Teddy's
paleobotboy
penis, once a
rallying cry,
now the anthem
of a lost cause.
Annoying false
close-up, during
these moments I
am herald of
all wounds—prosody
or revulsion.

Clear moon-ripped night
or a red-haired
hacienda.
Danni turned the
fleshlight off, the
creative powers
of slumber. Or
do they lack an
ethnicity
or running water?
Always unsmile
or wash away
the leftover
years of rice, the
Long Macho into
history. James
Goldofini
with a power
blue chemise is
dyingnamite
as uncontested
Scotch. Or he
reached for the light
a second time.

You knew of an
antithetical
person. Excessive
voiceover needs
damage with a
happy ending,
a creamathon
image. I was
twenty-two for
most of my adult
life. It's important
to have goats or
some rust collector
on the leaves of
dead trees. *Here* is
the time for the
syllable. *Here*
is its homeland
pain, the way rape
makes a system
by the west. A
barbed wire might
find me unfounded,
a man with an

unrestricted
personality.
You become a
grid who swims under
water, or the
wide waste of ocean-
breath empathy.
Octopus with
no sauce in a
dizzying cause.
Frilly testicles
of crisp fried squid.
Dishes bowl for
the afterlife.
When you lose your
place don't lose your
power: rapture
existential.
The forest was
dark or the half-
moron lighted
the foam, his mouth
an open beacon.
Interview with

the Common Cold,
be my generic.
The freedom of
stepping off the
bus. Nastagram,
creaking clothing,
inexorable
titles, discharged
deities. The
gold foil facade
evilly moves
to usefulness
of a grammar.
The entire world
of SHE apples
to me—they carve
their way towards Meg,
Tilly or Sadly,
piercing the porno
nighttime. Look at
me imploding
exponentially
like a pudding.
The archive of

experience
is freezing its
craving memory,
a face being
pushed by a cock.
Good offences
make good neighbors.
Opinion freedom:
a few medals
painted to my
chest. Little my
tragedy. The
rest of the world
is bored into
impotence of
recreational
math. Or the old
skulls resulting
from long study
of word problems:
WE INITIATE
WE BREAKUP.
Or the tiny
soundtrack quietly

worshipping the
same consonants
running an eternal
errand. Is Frank
Stella's mother
finally proud?
What's on at the
Cum? *Say Hi!—Stay
Hard!* Pre-Christian
delivery
service descramble
the egg someone
befalls me. Chaos
the most beautiful
music, as I
thought death into
existence. Soldiers
of Time am a
single living
stone or a good
sun becoming.
Dumbass façade,
tenants have ticks.
There's nothing so

sincere as waste.
Lugging video
equipment or
canaries, St.
Something dislikes
honesty, grew
up in Scarland.
Clouds make me angry,
a salty or
signifying
release. I try
undetermine
X-rated mattress.
Hemorrhoids are
the next phase of
A.I. The two
terms are running
practically
unexposed. A
South African
is beheading
home unjustly.
Ladies and Gestures,
I'm back at my

gay marble desk.
Are you free of
the universe?
The drawers don't
clothes. Shopping at
the tip of the
hill, she looks at
me from the corn
bears of her eyes.
A Measure in
Florida Claims
Black Solar Power.
Redefining
pain (again), attend
the closet mutant
to oscillate
between legs in
a spasm of body
shape—that water
exists only
in the form of
vapor, stone, or
sky. Or confront
a cruel tattoo

without seduction—
ejected a
member of the
House from Wyoming.
Not unentitled,
she pivoted
her sex on my
hand. The inner
world fluttered
against my mouth
and smelled easily.
It was a panic,
dark trees around
us. Or I heard
a noise or a
fish caught my eye.
Unfortunating
male, really,
how do we speak?
Death rises and
mingles with the
smoke rising through
the peaceful wind-
soaked trees. Frail

Hispanicide
army passing
through an exotic
magazine or
retrograte into
the accidental
zone, an extremely
common zero.
Little morbid
rugs smiling or
smartly wrought of
custom runaway
pieces. Official
liar, I'd better
reach you before
the prewashing,
a bill so sad
it's awesome. Who
knows what far-off
rights causes the
desert to think,
"This reasonable
music for me
to consider."

Date for Aliens
Who Overwhelm
the Fussy Toaster-
Ovens of their
Private Captors,
the surrealist
majority.
The false note of
a permanent
self, gargantuan
strawberry. There
was a group at
Columbia
called students making
it more expensive
for the upper
case while I pray
to the god of
this sentence. The
effects of the
grin had climaxed
the gist of his
trust. First thought best
thought LOL.

He left me but
also entered
me. We climbed among
the indistinct
plants. He had bored
stubby hands, sex
interrogated.
Triple gay guy
Eric Clapton
will play a pair
of shadows. Derail
the plan to Doctor
Cohen. Rain or cold
handmade the street
a theory of
sublime factory,
a shall-we-wave-
before-she-leaves
umbilical
indescribabilia.
Detonation
pre-trial, I am
loosing the coinage
to find round forms

from broad heart. Or
a lite snow was
feeling life's Plan
B: fuck luck. Even
a line of text
is a long narrow
bed where covers
are completely
deserted—etched
in shades of gay.
Benin bedroom
community
of Silicone
Valley. Or the
Norwellian
organization
for asylum
seekers. Or does
property, honor,
or character
matter? Are art
classes for the
undeserved youth
moved by my

delicacy
over what is
very wicked?
"Reality
is worse"—Flaubert.
My Godliness
is consciousness—
boundless or self-
deteriorating
by the light of
sterile candle
sticks. Remarkable
pomposity
for structures that
convey or connect.
Gag of battle,
she is in a
sense the ingenious
sneak that cloud drapes
autumn, decanter
of animal world,
infamous "now"
of recognizability.
I soaked my head

in the caffè
latte, random
shades of glass in
a little pitch
blue. I word banal
cheat-sheets for an
illiterate.
I know all mountains
say their children
are sweet. White people
were making yoghurt
before they were
invented. Ghosts
are often dead-
ended by offers,
the annual
stampede sale
in many cases
gratified right
into them through
attenuations.
There's unrelated
poetry to
solve, reknowned but

not widely. The
Federal Election
Commission of
Common Sense: Even
the good bombers
are not safe as
Gostar's birthdate
slows down. Who is
sleeping eating
or speaking, who?
Necessary
good? Check this out:
do people need
reason to be
dumb?—incidents
of moral slapstick?
Or will people
find a code in
divination?
The criminal
crab season, I
sat on a beach
in the museum,
families lying

out on colossal
towels, flesh-eating
flesh. Breathe into
history with
your wet mouth, that
intricately
corrupt primal
real estate. How
to bulletproof
your child? Be your
own Hamlet, his
zit for life. He
was a rubble
without a cause,
a symbolton.
To write unruly
is to speak from
the depths. He found
his historical
ache in the life
of red bricks with
their hemorrhaging
pattern. Big business
of the unconscious

survived a hundred
teen boys' outrages
to property.
Theology
makes dating more
complicated,
the detection
of the cosmic
weirdos, a seat
at the table
wearing a special
hat that highlights
her dancer's legs.
Tetsumi Kudo's
sculptures damage
the world. Or
I became the
eggplant in the
room, a new way
to learn more sincere
data at the
Coroner's Office.
Intervention
of a woman

of means by a
machine. Let my
cup passeth the
ongoing
test. Or improve
sick dictator
but victory
is simply a
slipping stone to
the big prize,
a gnostic punch,
a death breathing
undulating
image of Hilma
af Klint. I, a
pestilent, take
temporary
vows living on
modest silence.

Acknowledgements:

Gratitude to *Where Eagles Dare, Harness, Zaza, The Recluse, Aufgabe, Elderly, Shampoo, Shiny, Denver Quarterly, Vanitas, X Poetics, 443PAS*, and the PIP (Project for Innovative Poetry) blog. Thank you Chris Komater, Loring McAlpine, and the Gesso Foundation.

Robert Glück served as director of San Francisco State University's The Poetry Center, co-director of Small Press Traffic Literary Center, and associate editor at Lapis Press. His books include two novels, *Jack the Modernist* and *Margery Kempe*, two books of stories, *Elements* and *Denny Smith*, a book of poems, *Reader*, and with Kathleen Fraser, a book of prose poems, *In Commemoration of the Visit.* With Bruce Boone, Glück translated La Fontaine for a book of that name. With Camille Roy, Mary Berger, and Gail Scott, he edited *Biting the Error: Writers on Narrative.* Glück prefaced *Between Life and Death*, a volume of Frank Moore's paintings, and, with artist Dean Smith, made the film *Aliengnosis*, based on readings from *I, Boombox*. Other books include *Communal Nude: Collected Essays*, and *Parables*, an editioned artist book with Cuban artists José Angel Toirac and Meira Marrero Díaz. *Margery Kempe* was republished by NYRB Classics in 2020 and his novel *About Ed* by NYRB in 2023.